Expel the Jezebel in Me

A 30-Day Devotional

Robyn and Brandi Cunningham

Expel the Jezebel in Me: A 30-Day Devotional
Copyright 2022 by Robyn and Brandi Cunningham

All rights reserved. No part of this book may be reproduced, stored in a retrieval system, or transmitted in any form or by any means-electronic, mechanical, photocopy, recording, or otherwise-without prior written permission of the copyright owner.

Scripture quotations marked NIV are taken from the Holy Bible, NEW INTERNATIONAL VERSION®, NIV® Copyright © 1973, 1978, 1984, 2011 by Biblica, Inc.® Used by permission. All rights reserved worldwide.

Scripture quotations marked KJV are taken from the King James Version of the Bible. Public domain in the USA.

All emphasis in scripture is author's own.

ISBN: 978-1-953143-04-4 (Print)

    978-1-953143-05-1 (E-book)

Printed in the USA.

Contents

Preface		5
Introduction: What's in a Name?		11
Day 1	Jezebel Controls and Manipulates	15
Day 2	Jezebel Instills Fear in Others	17
Day 3	Jezebel Exhibits Insecurity	19
Day 4	Jezebel Feels Rejected	21
Day 5	Jezebel Seeks Attention	23
Day 6	Jezebel Seeks Titles or Positions	25
Day 7	Jezebel Exhibits Passive Aggressiveness	27
Day 8	Jezebel Exhibits Seductiveness	29
Day 9	Jezebel Exhibits Selfishness	31
Day 10	Jezebel is Performance Minded	33
Day 11	Jezebel Has Religious or Pharisaical Tendencies	35
Day 12	Jezebel has Cunning or Sly Tendencies	37
Day 13	Jezebel has a Rescue or Savior Complex	39
Day 14	Jezebel Has False Humility	41
Day 15	Jezebel Exhibits Fakeness	43
Day 16	Jezebel Brings Division	45
Day 17	Jezebel Demands Compliance	47
Day 18	Jezebel Becomes Defensive When Confronted	49
Day 19	Jezebel Seeks Relationships with Ahabs	51
Day 20	Jezebel Allows the Holy to Become Defiled	53

Day 21 Jezebel Worships Idols	55
Day 22 Jezebel Is Driven by Self	57
Day 23 Jezebel Promotes Her Agenda, Doesn't Meet Needs	59
Day 24 Jezebel Answers to "No One but God"	61
Day 25 Jezebel Operates in New Age Teachings	63
Day 26 Jezebel Attempts to Make Things Happen in Her Own Ability	65
Day 27 Jezebel Needs to be Needed by Others	67
Day 28 Jezebel Seeks to Reap Harvest Field Planted by Others	69
Day 29 Jezebel Operates Using Unauthorized Authority	71
Day 30 Conclusion	73

Preface

Jezebel is a topic of which every person in the church should be aware. It is evident, in this day and age, that the spirit of Jezebel is running rampant in our country, on our TVs, in our music, in our schools, and almost everywhere you look around you. What if I told you that the Jezebel spirit might not be just in the world around you, but could be influencing your actions from the dark areas of your soul in which you haven't allowed Jesus to shine His light?

This devotional will be a tool that encourages anyone to see Jezebellic tendencies in themselves or in members of their fellowship. Christians will be able to use this devotional to help guide themselves or others to freedom, without just throwing a label out there with no solution. This way no one will be left hanging by an accusation, but are also given a tool to utilize, in order be set free. In this devotional, you will go through the process for thirty days, of praying to recognize, expose, and expel these traits.

A typical church member is often very good at labeling a person, accusing a person, or somehow (whether intentionally, or unintentionally) slandering a person with the label of Jezebel and then abandoning them. They are left reeling in agony trying to discern if they truly are Jezebellic in nature or if they are just misguided or spiritually immature, and in need of some help getting free from those strongholds.

If you are a person who has laid blame on someone for being a Jezebel, thought in your heart that someone is operating in a spirit of Jezebel, or are someone who has been wounded by the label of a Jezebel and haven't been able to be healed, then this devotional is for you. It is time that you get set free and learn the tools so you can help others be free as well.

Expel the Jezebel in Me

This devotional is a tool for those who want to enter positions of authority in the body of Christ, at work, or at home. It is not only for leadership, but also for anyone seeking greater levels of purity in their walk with God. Anyone in the body of Christ that wants to have the closest possible relationship with God that they can have.

This is the verse that inspired me to seek my own freedom in Christ when I was accused of this very same thing:

> Search me, God, and know my heart; test me and know my anxious thoughts. See if there is any offensive way in me and lead me in the way everlasting. (Psalm 139: 23-24 NIV)

As members of the body of Christ, we can't deal with Jezebel in our nation, jobs, family, community, etc. if we are not pure ourselves. You can use this devotional as a tool to create a reflective time between you and the Lord to say, "Lord, please expose this in me so that I can take authority over it in my life. Help me learn to lead others into freedom and authority over this as well. Lead me in the way everlasting."

In order for this devotional to really work for you and make a profound, deep, lasting impact in your life, we need to identify what a Jezebel spirit is. By-and-large we are taught by the church the Jezebel is a spirit of lust and seduction, but there is much more to this foul spirit than meets the eye.

It's important to establish that operating in a Jezebellic manner does not mean that you are possessed by a demon. These are traits that both men and women can operate in. Jezebellic tendencies are the result of influence coming from an anti-Christ spirit, which is to say, anything that is not in line with what Christ says is how Christians should act, or anything that exalts itself against the knowledge of God.

Signs and symptoms, you are operating in a Jezebellic spirit:

- Manipulating issues for your benefit.
- Making things happen in your own power.

- Manipulating others to join you to accomplish your own agenda.
- Being protective over yourself and others in an unhealthy manner (controlling).
- Retaliating when rejected.
- Being overly spiritual and religious with everything in an exaggerated manner.
- Isolating and pitting people against each other; saying this person said that, and that person said that.
- Being self-defensive and redirecting accusations towards others, shifting blame from yourself.
- Playing the victim, never accepting responsibility for your actions.
- Not being accountable to anyone, or pretending like you are and doing what you want anyway, then accusing others of being a *Jezebel*.
- Accusing people falsely and with no substance, and when confronted (if no evidence is provided to the contrary) accusing the one confronting of having their own agenda.
- Attaching yourself to leadership in order to gain favor.
- Acting like you are more discerning than others.
- Attacking the spiritual fruit of believers.
- Straight up lying about others.
- Gossiping
- Slandering

Consequences if you tolerate and allow Jezebellic tendencies to operate in yourself and others.

- It creates divisions.
- Believers are unable to fully walk in their calling because they are trying to make something happen, which will prevent God from being able to operate how He wants.
- It will hinder others walk with God.
- It will prevent others from getting a promotion (spiritual or physical).

- It will traumatize and wound others.
- It will taint the body of Christ.
- It can accidentally create idol worship and the consequences thereof.
- It will prevent the flow of God.
- It will destroys marriages among many other things that can be detrimental to our lives and those around us.

Signs you are being targeted by a Spirit of Jezebel or are sitting under a Jezebellic authority:

- Irrational fear
- Confusion and distrust
- Sickness and infirmity
- Unusual exhaustion for no known reason
- Some form of perversion attempts to access your life, dreams, or thoughts.
- Forgetfulness, prone to making mistakes, and unusual occurrences – these things become so common that you think, "Why bother? Something bad is going to happen anyway."
- Isolation from everyone
- Withdrawal and wanting to be alone
- No motivation to work, no drive for your passions in life
- Attacks on your finances
- Spiritual lethargy
- Attacks on relationships in your family
- Feelings of worthlessness; feeling unvalued
- Feelings of rejection
- Feelings of inadequacy
- Feeling like prayers aren't being answered
- Words and sentences getting twisted
- People can't receive what you are trying to communicate; You will hear something others didn't say or vice versa.
- Increased dreams of being attacked by spiders, octopi, squid, or anything with many arms or "a hand in everything"

- Leadership that is very detailed oriented in a controlling manner, being micromanaged with unnecessary cause.
- Not being allowed to operate or hindered from operating in the gifts and callings of the Holy Spirit in a controlling, ungodly manner.

Introduction: What's in a Name?

When I hear the word or even the name *Jezebel*, I immediately have an image or idea of some licentious woman with no morals, no respect for authority unless it benefits her, a worshiper of false idols, etc. Seldom, if ever, do I think of a normal person or a Christian who is operating in such behaviors.

Truth be told, it's not that uncommon for Christians to operate in a Jezebellic manner. If we boil it down to its simplest context, a Jezebellic nature is a nature of manipulation and control. Typically, we see this as a self-defense mechanism that stems from past traumas that we haven't dealt with.

Have you ever heard the phrase coined by Shakespeare, "What's in a name?" In the epic monologue by Romeo, he questions if a rose would still be a rose if it were called by any other name? To answer his question, biblically speaking, yes, it would cease to be a rose.

We must look at this through the lens of the book of Genesis and a Hebraic mindset. The Hebrew understanding of a name is that it identifies the nature and characteristics of something or someone. In the second chapter of Genesis, God brought all the animals to Adam to be named,

> And Adam gave names to all cattle, and to the fowl of the air, and to every beast of the field; but for Adam there was not found an help meet for him. (Genesis 2:20 KJV)[1]

---

1. "Genesis 2 (KJV) - And Adam gave names to." Blue Letter Bible. Accessed 13 Feb, 2022. https://www.blueletterbible.org/kjv/gen/2/20/s_2020

Expel the Jezebel in Me

Adam named them all. For example, Adam named the serpent a nachash.[2] Then when we look at the same word in Strong's 5172,[3] we see it means "to practice divination, a sorcerer, to observe signs, to hiss, whisper, prognosticate (perform magic), learn by experience, diligently observe." Later, God calls Satan an ancient serpent in Revelation 20:2. In this instant, knowing the alternative meanings of snake in Hebrew, we see that Satan and his servants do in fact exhibit the characteristics of the name serpent that was given in the garden.

We see that the Hebrew people understood the power of the name in how they named people. Moses drew out the Hebrew people from Egypt and his name meant to draw out. He was also drawn out of the River Nile. Jesus' name means "Yahweh is Salvation" and God brought us salvation through him. We see this time and time again in the Bible.

So, what's in the name *Jezebel*? No one really knows what the name means, but some speculate it means "Where is my Lord?" Some think it means "pure or virginal." However, from a biblical standpoint, those were never the case.

I have discovered that if you take any word in the Bible and translate the original Proto-Hebraic symbols into definitions based off the symbolism of their original pictographs, as well as the numerical value and meanings associated with each symbol, you discover hidden messages, and characteristics in the letter's definitions.

The word *Jezebel* in spelled *aleph, yud, zayin, beit, lamed.*

The original pictograph of *Aleph* was a bull's head. This letter represents power, strength, the ox, chief, or ruler. When used at the beginning of a Hebrew word, it can represent a singular future tense of "I will."

---

2. "H5175 - nāḥāš - Strong's Hebrew Lexicon (kjv)." Blue Letter Bible. Accessed 13 Feb, 2022. https://www.blueletterbible.org/lexicon/h5175/kjv/wlc/0-1/

3. "H5172 - nāḥaš - Strong's Hebrew Lexicon (kjv)." Blue Letter Bible. Accessed 13 Feb, 2022. https://www.blueletterbible.org/lexicon/h5172/kjv/wlc/0-1/

The original pictograph of *Yud* was a closed hand. This letter represents the hand, to work, to throw, divine order, blessing, judgment, a portion or tithe.

The original pictograph of *Zayin* was a plowshare, sword, and arm. This letter represents the idea of, to adorn, cut, feed, complete, wholeness.

The original pictograph of *Beit* was a tent. This letter represents a house, family, divide, oppose, judge, discern, to witness, sons and daughters.

The original pictograph of *Lamed* was a shepherds hook or staff. This letter represents leadership, a perfect government, order, teaching, learning, protection, goad, yoke, and bind.

By putting these definitions together, we see both the good and the bad aspects of this name hidden in the definitions and symbolic representations of the name.

Jezebel's story and identity would read as such:

> Born to be a leader and a ruler. She was meant to bring divine order or blessings. When not operating in her purest calling, she operates with a closed fist and brings judgment. She can usher in peace or war and operates in a double portion of strength. She raises a family that either breaks the yoke or oppresses the witnesses.

All these possible meanings are displayed by Jezebel at various times in her life. She was a leader, the queen of Israel. She united the prophets of Baal and the country of Israel under worship to Baal. She bore false witness in a vicarious manner against Naboth and hired others to lie about him so she would steal his vineyard. She brought judgment on the land of Israel and put a heavy yoke on the people through her disobedience to God.

She truly did live up to her name. Unfortunately, she displayed more of the negative aspects than the positive ones. She was controlling, manipulative, and a harsh ruler. Sadly, a large portion of Christians operating in some of these traits as well and don't ever recognize it. Let's delve into that in this devotional.

Day 1

Jezebel Controls and Manipulates

How is this manifested in everyday life?
- Passive Aggressiveness. Making "jokes" that are not really jokes.
- Suggests someone do something for us when we don't want to do it.
- Complains about sickness to get attention.
- Attempts to control the way someone thinks.
- Obsesses over something or someone.
- Causes someone to feel a certain emotion so we can get our way.
- Has an agenda for oneself and not making it known from the beginning.
- Has things to hide.

Record your thoughts below.

Do I do this in any way?

_____
_____
_____
_____
_____

If so, what is my motive?

_____

_____

_____

_____

_____

_____

Pray with me through the expelling of this trait:

Lord, I have been wrong to cross others' boundaries or boundaries that I know shouldn't be crossed. I believe You are healing me from all fears that would fill me with tendencies to act any or all these ways. I truly desire to make You and Your agenda my one and only focus. Help me to truly learn Your heart for others' so that I can promote them instead of me, and so I can understand the situation. Help me to immediately recognize the triggers that try to lead me back into operating in the old ways of control and manipulation. I know that is the old man and that part of me died with Jesus on the cross. I trust You, Father.

Day 2

Jezebel Instills Fear in Others

How is this manifested in everyday life?

- Threatens to demote another from a position or status held in a relationship.
- Punishes with fear. Withholding affection/attention to punish or with a child spanking.
- Tells children bedtime stories to scare them to make them stay in their beds.
- Conditionally loves. Example, stating children will not get presents if they are not good.
- Belittles others and complains, instilling fear into the atmosphere.
- Shuts down all communication if someone says something that hits you the wrong way.
- Interrogates and probes for details to teach others they are right.

Record your thoughts below.

Do I do this in any way?

_____
_____
_____
_____
_____
_____

If so, what is my motive?

_____

_____

_____

_____

_____

_____

Pray with me through the expelling of this trait:

Lord, You have not loved me conditionally. You always use Your words to encourage and not criticize. You are Love, and love sees the best in all people, all the time. You are the most life-giving and trustworthy being I know. You instill trust in everyone who allows You to change them, including me. Father, I want to be like You, and I want to love others unconditionally and encourage them. I want to bring abundance into every atmosphere I'm in, as well as give others a platform from which to succeed instead of planting fear in them. Please destroy all the negative things I have said and forgive me for every way I have operated in negativity and fear.

Day 3

Jezebel Exhibits Insecurity

How is this manifested in everyday life?

- Seeks relationships with those in higher positions so that if anyone else finds out their agenda, they won't be affected due to their own created "self-favor."
- Again, belittles others.
- Feels the need to cover one's tracks.
- Does more talking than listening.
- Often seeks approval. Compromises one's values to please someone else.

Record your thoughts below.

Do I do this in any way?

_____
_____
_____
_____
_____
_____
_____
_____

If so, what is my motive?

_____

_____

_____

_____

_____

_____

Pray with me through the expelling of this trait:

Lord, I ask right now that You reveal my heart's motives. Reveal to me any area I am insecure and may be displaying traits of insecurity. I know that my hope is found in You alone, and my confidence is found in You alone. I want You to be the only person I want to please. I want You to be the only person I seek approval from. I repent right now for ever having used anyone to get something I want. I repent for belittling anyone. I repent for giving anyone else the power over me to be able to cause me to feel negative emotions. I turn from believing lies and say from this moment forward, I walk in Your truth.

Day 4

Jezebel Feels Rejected

How is this manifested in everyday life?

- Feels like wanting to hide in a corner or in a closet.
- Feels invisible or isolated.
- Makes plans with others and they often get cancelled.
- Longs just to have acknowledgement from leaders.
- Often goes through everyday feeling numb.
- Occasionally may have thoughts of suicide.
- Hope is deferred and the fire of passion feels put out.

Record your thoughts below.

Do I do this in any way?

_____
_____
_____
_____
_____
_____
_____
_____

If so, what is my motive?

_____

_____

_____

_____

_____

_____

Pray with me through the expelling of this trait:

Jesus, my brother! Thank You that You always have arms wide open! You are the giver of life, not the One who takes it away! You don't deny me; You want and desire me! Forgive me for believing the lies of rejection when Your truth is the only truth I should allow myself to live in. Right now, I break the power rejection has over me, in Jesus' mighty name. I declare that I am wanted, accepted, valued, loved, desired, and so much more! I thank You, Jesus, for ridding me of the isolation that the enemy tries so diligently to get me to live in, so that I won't get out there and be You to the people in my life.

Day 5

Jezebel Seeks Attention

How is this manifested in everyday life?

- Wears clothes that show a little too much and enjoys being "looked at."
- Is loud and boisterous.
- Always has something to say.
- Feels the need to, "One up," others in conversations.
- Gives others advice through the perspective that you completely understand what the other is going through.
- Always on the look out to see who is watching, even during worship time at church.
- Offers solutions to others' problems that are not yours to solve.

Record your thoughts below.

Do I do this in any way?

_____
_____
_____
_____
_____
_____
_____

Expel the Jezebel in Me

If so, what is my motive?

_____
_____
_____
_____
_____
_____

Pray with me through the expelling of this trait:

Father God, You know me. You know that there are areas of attention seeking that I struggle with, as we all do. I lay them ALL at Your feet NOW, and I take up Your perfect peace in place of the fear of not being given attention or love. I forgive all of those who have hurt me in the past; knowingly or unknowingly. I bind myself to You. I declare I have Holy Spirit blinders on me, so that I can only focus on You and what You're doing. I only want to "go where my Father goes, and to do what my Father does." I ask that You help me recognize today any of these things I do so that I can ask myself, "Where's God?" and "What is He focused on?" so I can be focused on that too.

Day 6

Jezebel Seeks Titles or Positions

How is this manifested in everyday life?
- Compromises values, thus compromising morals to obtain favor. - Practically this looks like staying at work later even though you know your family is waiting for you at home, and family should come first.
- Gives children sweets and takes them to do things because you know it will cause them to like you more, even though you know it's not what is best for them at the time.
- Desires to be a pastor or leader because the pastor/leader often is viewed as the one that gets to, "rescue," everyone, and is the one most go to for advice.
- Seeks position of educator so they can implement their own hidden agenda with programming others.

Record your thoughts below.
Do I do this in any way?

_____
_____
_____
_____
_____

If so, what is my motive?

_____
_____
_____
_____
_____
_____

Pray with me through the expelling of this trait:

Lord, even though this is hard, right now I ask You to take me out of every position I am in with a title that is not Your will for me to be in, no matter how messy that might look. I ask You to teach me how to strengthen myself in Your Word. That way, when Satan tries to get me to compromise my values, I can see him for what he's doing and not participate. I ask that You bless every leader that I have cursed. I repent for thinking I should be the one teaching, and acting in jealousy without giving regard to the fact that it may not be the position for me at this time, or that it could affect many people negatively for me to step into something that it is not my time to step in to.

Day 7

Jezebel Exhibits Passive Aggressiveness

How is this manifested in everyday life?
- Makes the new person at work do all the hard things because you don't want to do them.
- Makes suggestions and then accuses someone of not doing what was asked of them when there were no formal directions given.
- Hints to someone that they want something done and not drawing clear boundaries.
- Tests boundaries/limits.
- Texts or messages when confrontation is needed but refuses to talk in person.
- Is two-faced. Is a wolf in sheep's' clothing. Builds someone up to his/her face, then slanders them behind their back.

Record your thoughts below.
Do I do this in any way?

_____
_____
_____
_____
_____

Expel the Jezebel in Me

If so, what is my motive?

_____

_____

_____

_____

_____

_____

Pray with me through the expelling of this trait:

Father, passive aggressiveness is not from You. You are open, truthful, and loving. You have pure motives, so there are no reasons to become passively aggressive. I ask that You purify me of any and all passive aggressive tendencies, and that You forgive me for operating in it and of any and all ways that I have participated in it in the past. I will cling tight to Your Word that says I have courage and strength and that You are with me where I go; that You will never leave or forsake me. I ask You to help me realize when I'm behaving in this way, and help me learn how to do the right thing at the right time. I trust You.

Day 8

Jezebel Exhibits Seductiveness

How is this manifested in everyday life?

- Wears an excessive amount of makeup, with the MOTIVE of alluring another.
- Pitches a good idea with bells and whistles but does not deliver what is promised.
- Works to convince someone they need to do something, because it's what is best for themselves, not because it's in the best interest of the other person.
- Says, "If you do this for me, I will do this for you."
- Makes promises they know they can't or won't be able to keep.
- Constantly feel the need to talk about everything they have accomplished.
- In interviews, acts like they are overqualified for the job because of everything they have done, but exaggerate a couple of things. Tells white lies.

Record your thoughts below.

Do I do this in any way?

_____
_____
_____

If so, what is my motive?

___

Pray with me through the expelling of this trait:

> *Lord, the world believes in conditional love. That is, "If I do something for you, you need to do something for me." This is not Your kingdom's ways. This is not unconditional love. Unconditional love doesn't brag about oneself; it is humble. Love doesn't lie. It only chooses to walk in the truth. Lord, I give You permission to reveal to me any of these areas that I may be walking in and declare I want You to help me overcome them. It's not easy, but with the Holy Spirit, my Helper, I can do it. Reveal to me any needs I'm not getting met that make me want to act these ways, and teach me how to get them met in righteous ways.*

Day 9

Jezebel Exhibits Selfishness

How is this manifested in everyday life?
- When there is a problem, offers a solution, but not *being* the solution.
- Takes conversations personal, only later to find out the conversation was never about them.
- Thinks others are talking about them when chattering is heard, but can't hear clearly what's being said.
- Expects something in return when you do good for someone else.
- Expects others to come to you and apologize first in relationships.
- Thinks about what they want to say next while someone else is talking.

Record your thoughts below.
Do I do this in any way?

_____
_____
_____
_____

Expel the Jezebel in Me

If so, what is my motive?

_____
_____
_____
_____
_____
_____

Pray with me through the expelling of this trait:

Lord, I have been selfish, as we all have. Thank You for pointing out the ways I have been or am operating in selfishness and removing them from me as far as the east is from the west! I desire to be more and more like You, drawing ever closer. I know these are bold prayers, but humble me, Lord, and make me completely selfless like You. Help me to listen to others, apologize first, and not make situations that are not about me, about me. Help me not to make up stories and lies and believe them, Lord. I declare I will see my actions as they are, and I will take full ownership for them from this day forward.

Day 10

Jezebel is Performance Minded

How is this manifested in everyday life?
- Thinks people are watching even during worship at church.
- Thinks people are talking about them when their conversation can't be heard.
- Seeks approval.
- Needs validation even once they have received it.
- Often feels overlooked. Needs constant words of encouragement.
- Needs an excessive number of hugs.
- Sings or expresses their talent and hopes someone hears or sees how well they are doing.

Record your thoughts below.
Do I do this in any way?

_____
_____
_____
_____
_____
_____

Expel the Jezebel in Me

If so, what is my motive?

_____
_____
_____
_____
_____
_____

Pray with me through the expelling of this trait:

Lord, I need You to reinforce to me that I AM the apple of Your eye. That I AM your precious daughter. That You love hearing, seeing, experiencing, and spending time with me. I need to be told by You how well I am doing, and I apologize for seeking that from anywhere but You. When I look in the mirror, I should see You in me. But I don't always see myself the way You see me. I am open and expecting to receive Your view of me today. Today, I turn from performance, receive forgiveness, and look forward to the new level of focus and confidence I have in You, as I am the apple of Your eye!

Day 11

Jezebel Has Religious or Pharisaical Tendencies

How is this manifested in everyday life?
- Holds oneself and others to false expectations.
- Is pious and dogmatic.
- Is unable to get out of routines without feeling grumpy.
- Judges people when they should be using discernment.
- Criticizes themself or others more than they encourage.
- Constantly being humbled or put in situations that show that they are not the one with the most knowledge.
- Convinces others of their argument about Jesus rather than hearing the concerns of others.

Record your thoughts below.
Do I do this in any way?

_____
_____
_____
_____
_____
_____

Expel the Jezebel in Me

If so, what is my motive?

_____
_____
_____
_____
_____
_____

Pray with me through the expelling of this trait:

Jesus, You are the WAY! Forgive me right now for thinking I know how to handle situations, what people should be doing, what they should be thinking, and how I should get to live my life. Remove from me all religious and dogmatic strongholds and attitudes that may reside in me. Please remove them far from me, never to return again. Help me to lead people to You, as You are the way, and You know how each person should live their own lives.

Day 12

Jezebel has Cunning or Sly Tendencies

How is this manifested in everyday life?
- Manipulates situations to accomplish their own will.
- Reaches out for advice from the person they know will give the answer that will make them feel good or aligns with what they want others to say during certain situations.
- Knows how to cover ones' tracks.
- Does not feel remorse when justifying sin.
- Ability to tell white lies without feeling guilty or can ignore the guilty feeling.
- Tends to not pay attention to details.

Record your thoughts below.
Do I do this in any way?

_____
_____
_____
_____
_____
_____
_____

If so, what is my motive?

_____
_____
_____
_____
_____
_____

Pray with me through the expelling of this trait:

Lord, straighten out all my ways. Change me so that I am always walking in purity one hundred percent of the time. Rid of me the desire to manipulate others through telling white lies, exaggerating, justifying sin, or seducing them. Help me to untangle the webs I have made and the tracks that I feel like I must cover up. I know that this may be a process, but I trust that, as long as I'm with You, I can face my fears and all things will be worked together for my good and the good of those involved. Please help me to love instead of hurt others by being cunning or sly. Thank You, Holy Spirit, for helping me.

Day 13

Jezebel has a Rescue or Savior Complex

How is this manifested in everyday life?
- Believe that people should come to them because they have the time and answer for everyone.
- Tries to meet all needs that they see that need to be met; even at the expense of sacrificing family time and/or resources, or even if it might cause one to compromise their values.
- Neglects their own needs to meet needs of others. I.E. Answers phone call to someone in need when they shouldn't answer at that time.
- Tries to be "Super Mom," "Super Wife," or, "Super _____."
- Disguises tolerating Jezebel as "loving" people.

Record your thoughts below.

Do I do this in any way?

_____
_____
_____
_____
_____
_____

Expel the Jezebel in Me

If so, what is my motive?

_____

_____
_____
_____
_____
_____

Pray with me through the expelling of this trait:

Lord, I know that You are the Savior. I know that You are the One who reveals the wisdom and knowledge people need to hear in moments of crisis. Help me to discern when I should and when I shouldn't assist someone who is going through a crisis or a reoccurring situation. Help me to know the difference between helping and enabling. Please reveal any people I keep in my life because they need me, or because I think I need them. Help me to see if I am being an intercessor for someone to make them feel like I am always there as a rescuer, or if it's because I am called to be there. I trust You with them, Holy Spirit; I trust You with all people. Help me to know my boundaries. Thank You!

Day 14

Jezebel Has False Humility

How is this manifested in everyday life?
- Is consumed with self-image and getting self needs met even though it looks like one is meeting the needs of others.
- Saying, "I'm just a _____," Not stating the true value of your identity in Christ.
- Makes known the sacrifices they made to serve someone else. *Especially their significant other.*
- Begs God instead of walking in the authority they have truly been given as Christians.
- Believes sickness is from God and remain in it.
- Believes God wants them to be in poverty in order to be a humble servant of Him.

Record your thoughts here.

Do I do this in any way?

_____
_____
_____
_____
_____

If so, what is my motive?

_____

_____

_____

_____

_____

_____

Pray with me through the expelling of this trait:

> *I repent for ever having accepted sickness as something I was meant to go through, as if I'm saying what Jesus did on the cross wasn't enough. I repent for ever being full of self-pity. I repent for not accepting the inheritance You may have for me in any way, shape, or form. Help me to see the truth for what it is and walk in the FULLNESS of Your kingdom, here on earth, Lord, so as to provoke Israel to jealousy! I desire for people to see You for who You really are, and not what my wrong mindset says You are. I give You permission to rid me of all false humility now, in Jesus' name.*

Day 15

Jezebel Exhibits Fakeness

How is this manifested in everyday life?
- Is unable to verbalize emotions and emotional needs.
- Appears happy on the outside yet dying on the inside.
- Explains the experience one can have without really having that much experience in a certain area. Have trouble finding fulfillment.
- Always doing things to improve their physical body, even at the cost of their own health.
- Tells people what they want to hear.
- Does not stand up for something and falls for everything.
- Naïve. Unable to connect to others on emotional and deep levels.

Record your thoughts below.
Do I do this in any way?

_____
_____
_____
_____

Expel the Jezebel in Me

If so, what is my motive?

_____

_____

_____

_____

_____

_____

Pray with me through the expelling of this trait:

God, I want to know You in a deeper way than I ever have! I also need Your help, God, with getting to know the emotions that I cover up, hide, or have a hard time feeling and expressing. Sometimes, Lord, I am double minded or fractured, and it causes me to behave differently in various situations with different people instead of remaining who I am in You consistently. I ask, Father, for You to heal every wounded area of my heart. Heal and deliver me from any oppression or depression. Set me up high so I can exalt You in front of others because of the healing You are bringing me that is making me whole.

Day 16

Jezebel Brings Division

How is this manifested in everyday life?

- Steps on others to, "move up the ladder."
- Plants seeds of negative words or rumors about other people; pitting one against another.
- Gets an unhealthy satisfaction of watching one's enemies fail.
- Creates confusion.
- Takes things that were said out of context.
- Manipulates what they hear to mean what they wanted to hear.
- Targets leadership and marriages to bring division.

Record your thoughts below.

Do I do this in any way?

_____
_____
_____
_____
_____
_____
_____

Expel the Jezebel in Me

If so, what is my motive?

_____
_____
_____
_____
_____
_____
_____

Pray with me through the expelling of this trait:

Lord, I know that these things are absolutely not of You, and I repent for ever having done anything to bring division, knowingly or unknowingly. I repent for ever having spoken negative words over a church or a married couple. I repent for speaking word curses over anyone's finances or jobs. Even if I believed I deserved a position more than the person who got it, I should never have said anything bad about them getting it. I know that it means You have a better position for me than the one I was hoping for. I break all seeds of division I have planted, and I declare I am a bringer and planter of unity.

Day 17

Jezebel Demands Compliance

How is this manifested in everyday life?
- Indirectly pushes for things to be done their own way.
- Treats others differently if their authority in a situation isn't respected.
- Controls and manipulates using documentation. Documents things that were assigned to one person but supposedly completed by another, then reports this to the authority stating the person didn't do what they were told to do. However, the person never really instructed CLEARLY what should have been done in the first place.
- Uses people and tries to cover it up by calling it, "Being a team player," but if there's resistance, they say to everyone, "This one is not a team player," and tries to shame you.

Record your thoughts below.
Do I do this in any way?

_____
_____
_____
_____
_____

If so, what is my motive?

___

Pray with me through the expelling of this trait:

Lord, I repent for having ever used a position to micromanage Your children. I repent for ever having been over detailed, or under detailed. I repent for anytime I have ever used information against someone that affected their life that truly had good intentions. I repent for ever having disciplined or shamed someone because they didn't do things the way I would have done them, even though they got the job done. I repent for using people's words against them when what they said was not supposed to be taken the way I took it, and I knew that but used it against them anyway. I release control to You!

Day 18

Jezebel Becomes Defensive When Confronted

How is this manifested in everyday life?
- Always has a reason for doing whatever they are being confronted for and will justify it all day.
- Talks more than listens. Draws conclusions or assumptions.
- Gets an attitude during difficult discussions.
- Rarely apologizes.
- Creates friendships/cliques out of offense.
- Fuels arguments instead of calms them.
- Is known to shut down or to have a temper.

Record your thoughts below.
Do I do this in any way?

_____
_____
_____
_____
_____
_____

If so, what is my motive?

_____
_____
_____
_____
_____
_____

Pray with me through the expelling of this trait:

We have all done these things at some point, Father. I admit to You that I was wrong to be defensive because confrontation, in reality, is just a conversation to try to reveal the truth in a situation, and if I'm walking in the truth, it shouldn't be something to be defensive about. I repent for not truly listening to others' concerns and assuming they are all going to treat me horribly during confrontation based on my negative experiences in the past. I repent for any time I should have apologized to someone, and I didn't. Humble me, Lord. I trust You. Thank You for setting me free from the fear of confrontation!

Day 19

Jezebel Seeks Relationships with Ahabs

How is this manifested in everyday life?
- Seeks connections with those who:
  - Tolerate evil instead of confronting it.
  - Are willing to "push things under the rug."
  - Are materialistic. Fires people or rids friendships for confronting or questioning them.
  - Are hypocritical: Sets boundaries and ethics for employees but allows corporate to go against those boundaries without consequences.
- Will go against the Stark Act in business for perks or referrals.
- Likes to flirt when it's not appropriate and gets away with it.

Record your thoughts below.

Do I do this in any way?

_____
_____
_____
_____

If so, what is my motive?

_____
_____
_____
_____
_____
_____

Pray with me through the expelling of this trait:

> *Forgive me for any time I sought out a position with a leader because I knew I would have perks other people didn't because I was the leader's friend. Forgive me for any time I flirted with a coworker when I knew it was against company ethics, policies, or just plain wasn't right. And forgive me as a leader for not shutting it down when I've seen it done in my sphere of influence. Forgive me for using my position with certain people to accomplish my hidden agenda. Forgive me for ever having a hidden agenda and not making that known from the beginning with new leaders over me.*

Day 20

Jezebel Allows the Holy to Become Defiled

How is this manifested in everyday life?

- Has sex before marriage.
- Brings others into marriage bed or partakes of porn, while married or unmarried.
- Allows demonic shows into their household.
- Does not take care of one's body.
- Allows homosexuality, abortion, etc. in the Body of Christ and does not stand up for the Truth when appropriate.
- Emotionally connects with those that are married and of the opposite sex without the other partner being present and mutually consenting to the relationship.
- Embraces compromising values or beliefs to fit in, for example, cussing when one doesn't normally.

Record your thoughts below.

Do I do this in any way?

_____
_____
_____
_____

Expel the Jezebel in Me

If so, what is my motive?

_____
_____
_____
_____
_____
_____
_____

Pray with me through the expelling of this trait:

This is a tough one, Jesus! I repent for having defiled the marriage bed or my intimacy with You at any point in time. I repent for not taking care of my own body, as I am the temple of the Holy Spirit. I repent for allowing foul language to come out of my mouth, as it not only defiles your temple, myself, but also the atmosphere in which I am speaking. I repent for not standing up for Your truth in situations where the opportunity has been presented for me to do so. I declare I am courageous, I am a messenger of Your Word, and I will stand up for what is right. I declare I am the righteousness of God.

Day 21

Jezebel Worships Idols

How is this manifested in everyday life?

- Chases after people that have the "anointing" of certain gifts to lay hands on and impart them to you. Jesus is The Anointing, and we all have the same Holy Spirit who is the One that administers the gifts.
- Always feels anxious or timid while around certain leaders.
- Struggles with people pleasing.
- Gets irritated when something they believe is being challenged.
- Thinks about themself above others.
- Being a workaholic.
- Does not seek to get free of strongholds or false doctrine beliefs.

Record your thoughts below.

Do I do this in any way?

___
___
___
___
___
___

Expel the Jezebel in Me

If so, what is my motive?

_____
_____
_____
_____
_____
_____

Pray with me through the expelling of this trait:

Lord, I want to be free of any and all known or unknown idol worship in my life right now! Deliver me of the fear of being in the presence of certain leaders, Lord! I don't know how to get free without You. Forgive me for any time I have done any of the things written about above. Help me to recognize that I need complete balance in my life and that balance starts with putting You first. Forgive me for putting busyness in life above my relationship with You. I love You, and I want to put You first in my life more than I ever have before. Help me to do this. I know You will!

Day 22

Jezebel Is Driven by Self

How is this manifested in everyday life?

- Takes situations into their own hands when they are not seeing the progress they think should be occurring.
- Sets goals without consulting God to see what His goals for their life is.
- Sets out to accomplish those goals with mind, will and emotions, and in their own strength.
- Overlooks the needs of others while on the journey to accomplish their goals.
- Boasts once goals are met.
- Leaves others behind that are taking too long to move forward with them.

Record your thoughts below.

Do I do this in any way?

_____
_____
_____
_____
_____
_____
_____

If so, what is my motive?

___

Pray with me through the expelling of this trait:

You made me to reach for goals, Father, but I want to set out to reach the goals You have set for me, and no other ones. I want to know when to race forward, yet also know how to deeply rest. I want to boast only in Your glory, and not about my own accomplishments, because my accomplishments are only able to be done because of all You have done for me. I lay my desires and goals down at Your feet, though it may seem hard, and I ask You to sift through the ones that are not of You, and return to me the ones that are. Thank You, for forgiving me, and for helping me to focus.

DAY 23

Jezebel Promotes Her Agenda, Doesn't Meet Needs

How is this manifested in everyday life?
- Has a subordinate that needs correction and they want to find a reason to dismiss them from the position, instead of teaching they are put on a, "plan of correction".
- Talks in circles instead of saying what needs to be said.
- Avoids answering questions directly or promptly solving problems.
- Confuse those listening to them speak.
- Finds a way to make their life better despite the cost.
- Withholds emotion or shuts down instead of nurturing communication.

Record your thoughts below.

Do I do this in any way?

_____
_____
_____
_____
_____

If so, what is my motive?

_____
_____
_____
_____
_____
_____

Pray with me through the expelling of this trait:

Father, we are all guilty of one or all of these traits at some point. For whatever reason, we tend to avoid giving direct answers or saying, "I don't know, let me find out," because of fear or insecurity, or out of defensiveness. Help me recognize when I am operating in these traits from this day forward, and heal and deliver me of any perversion or twisting of communication. I want what needs to be heard, be heard, and all confusion to be out of my life and the lives of those I impact, because Satan is the author of confusion, and I do not want to partner with him in any way, shape, or form. Thank You, Lord!

DAY 24

Jezebel Answers to "No One but God"

How is this manifested in everyday life?
- Does not seek wise counsel for fear of rejection of what they want to do.
- Does not want anyone, be it spouse, friend, etc. to hold them accountable for their actions.
- Gives prophetic words but doesn't receive them well.
- Doesn't have transparency in all areas of life.
- Lacks being detail-oriented.
- Counselor to all, patient or client to none.
- Fears being asked about details.

Record your thoughts below.
Do I do this in any way?

_____
_____
_____
_____
_____
_____
_____

If so, what is my motive?

_____
_____
_____
_____
_____
_____

Pray with me through the expelling of this trait:

Lord, forgive me for the times when I didn't want to be held accountable by anyone but You. I know that sometimes it is very hard to trust people, but I know that I can trust You with the people You have placed in my life. Help me to realize that true accountability, that is not used to shame, is a part of unconditional love. Help me see that I will not be criticized when I am found doing something I shouldn't have been, but that I will be supported and encouraged to get back on track. Forgive me for any time I have lacked in detail to hide something so as to, "Not lie, but not tell what's going on either."

Day 25

Jezebel Operates in New Age Teachings

How is this manifested in everyday life?
- Practices yoga.
- Partakes in "vibes," teaches or practices energy channeling
- Anointing sucking.
- Practices in superstitions. White witchcraft.
- Practices mind control. Goes to psychics. Participates in Halloween.
- Participates in Karate. Believes in spirit animals. Owns dream catchers.
- Participates in tarot card readings and/or horoscopes.

Record your thoughts below.
Do I do this in any way?

_____
_____
_____
_____
_____
_____
_____

Expel the Jezebel in Me

If so, what is my motive?

_____
_____
_____
_____
_____
_____

Pray with me through the expelling of this trait:

Lord, there are so many ways new-age beliefs have entered the church, and I know now that it is witchcraft. Please reveal Your truth to me about each of the things listed above, and any other thing in my life I may be holding on to that has roots in witchcraft. Forgive me for tainting Your Holy Place with witchcraft in my life at any point. Free me and others around me from the effects of any of these things I have participated in, and create a clean heart within me, Lord.

Day 26

Jezebel Attempts to Make Things Happen in Her Own Ability

How is this manifested in everyday life?
- Finds time to spend with the people in power but doesn't have much time for other coworkers.
- Seeks attention.
- Works seven days a week or over time, even though we are commanded to delight in the Sabbath.
- Does not tithe.
- Has a hard time trusting others or delegating tasks.
- Jeopardizes care for self to "get done what needs to get done."

Record your thoughts below.

Do I do this in any way?

_____
_____
_____
_____

If so, what is my motive?

_____
_____
_____
_____
_____
_____

Pray with me through the expelling of this trait:

Father, forgive me for ever putting things that need to get done, goals that need to be met, or bills that need to be paid, above You. You are Jehovah Jireh, my Provider. You are my Source and the One who gives me favor with the people I need in my life to get to where You are wanting me to go. Forgive me for any time I have given in to working overtime due to me wanting to be a people pleaser or in seeking a position, when I know I have personal needs, a family that needs to be taken care of at home, or prior commitments. Forgive me for any time I have given my word and not stuck to it due to needing to work overtime to please my boss/spouse.

Day 27

Jezebel Needs to be Needed by Others

How is this manifested in everyday life?
- Their circle of friends are those who come when they are experiencing a difficulty.
- Constantly telling others they can always be counted on, but behind the scenes others feel deep down that they didn't need to be helped this time.
- Refrain from sharing all the details with someone so that others still have a reason to need them. Yes, this also applies in business. Our job is to give freely and trust God.
- Constantly filling positions that are needed in the church, despite whether they have heard God call them or not. This goes closely with rescuing.
- Tries to pull others into positions they are not ready for, so that they can, "raise them up."

Record your thoughts below.
Do I do this in any way?

_____
_____
_____
_____

If so, what is my motive?

Pray with me through the expelling of this trait:

Lord, I repent for ever having pulled someone into a position I needed them in at work, at church, or in my life when I knew they didn't fully know what they were getting in to. I repent for using others to fill a position just because they were willing, when I knew it was not necessarily where they were called to be at that time in their life. Forgive me for not severing friendships that I should have severed long ago because I thought I needed them or they need me in their lives. Forgive me for not teaching my successor how to fully do my job and withholding any information that might be needed.

DAY 28

Jezebel Seeks to Reap Harvest Field Planted by Others

How is this manifested in everyday life?
- Gets offered a position with a new company or ministry but does not want to take it until the business is stable. Once someone else has taken the position and works until the business is stable, then they show interest in the position. Also by keeping your relationships with those in charge, they worm their way in no matter how it effects the others' that worked to grow the company/ministry/etc.
- Seeks handouts but knows they could get out there and work for what it is they are seeking.
- Markets to sites you are a part of that were founded and consistently built up by someone else.

Record your thoughts below.
Do I do this in any way?

_____
_____
_____
_____

Expel the Jezebel in Me

If so, what is my motive?

_____

_____

_____

_____

_____

_____

Pray with me through the expelling of this trait:

Lord, forgive me for waiting until others have worked hard to make something great before I decide to step in and help out. Forgive me for ever having worked to take someone's ministry, position, or influence that they worked so diligently or hard to get. Forgive me for ever having crossed boundaries to give prophetic words when I didn't have the authority to prophesy to members of a congregation. Forgive me for ever trying to promote my own business at someone else's event. Forgive me for ever having trash-talked another person or company so I could promote my own agenda.

Day 29

Jezebel Operates Using Unauthorized Authority

How is this manifested in everyday life?

- Jumps in front of someone or makes your own way to get into the lane you want to be in while driving, even though that spot is not being offered to you.
- Corrects someone that they are not formally positioned over or that has not given permission to speak into their life.
- Doesn't hear when others' set a boundary or gets defensive when boundaries are set.
- Takes for themselves a title that has not been given to them.
- Uses their friends' names to get in with someone or in to something, instead of earning it or allowing God to favor them on their own.

Record your thoughts below.

Do I do this in any way?

_____
_____
_____
_____
_____

Expel the Jezebel in Me

If so, what is my motive?

_____
_____
_____
_____
_____
_____

Pray with me through the expelling of this trait:

Open my ears, God! I want to be able to recognize when boundaries are set so I don't cross them. I want to be respectful of others and not push my will or what I think is right upon any of them. Forgive me for judging others' lives when I am not called to worry about how someone else lives their life, but to worry about how I live my own. Forgive me for giving unwanted or unasked for advice. Forgive me for ever having said I have any qualifications that I know I do not truly have. Forgive me for ever lying during an interview. Help me to listen to the needs of others and just strive to be You to all the people I meet, not to be a title.

DAY 30

Conclusion

As you can now tell, there are numerous ways in which Jezebellic spirit can manifest through you or someone you love. The intent of this devotional was to inform and educate you on the powerful and realistic tendencies that we can all operate in, knowingly or unknowingly, on a daily basis. It is through the healing of the Holy Spirit that we can become set free from our past and begin our journey towards wholeness. Wholeness is how we prevent ourselves from falling prey to these types of tendencies. Sometimes these are learned behaviors, and we still need accountability and love from a community of believers. Those who will love unconditionally to help us work through those behaviors. Thank you for taking the time to read and work through this book and I hope and believe that this devotional has opened your eyes so that each person reading this can now be more understanding when we see someone that is operating in or under a spirit of Jezebel.

This is book one of three in a series of devotionals. The next devotional will be to recognize the signs of Jezebel operating in our friends and family. It will walk you through prayers of release for them. The third and final book in this series will be on recognizing how Jezebel is working in our nation and how to unite together in prayer and dispel that spirit from our land that is one nation, under God!

For more information on Jezebel, or to seek out Brandi and Robyn for a healing session of having ever been called a Jezebel, or to leave a testimony of how this book has helped you, please visit our website at www.FiresideGrace.com.

About the Authors

Robyn and Brandi Cunningham are the founders of Fireside Grace, which was birthed to help individuals, ministries, and cities live to their full potential through Christ-based discipleship. Using the gifts of the Spirit, they teach truth to bring clarity to the body of Christ on issues that seem confusing in this modern age. They have a YouTube channel called Fireside Grace Ministries.

The Cunningham's goal to is to guide the church body by connecting the ethics, values, character, and morals of our ancestors into the present and future generations by creatively bringing the wisdom of the past, the wisdom of the Ancient of Days, and the wisdom of our elders into the present—and bridging the gaps of the generations in between. Together, Robyn and Brandi cover topics such as current issues, dream interpretation, learning how to hear God's voice, anointing, slaying sacred cows, and much more.

Robyn and Brandi are ordained under Michael French with Patria Ministries. They have been involved with various areas of ministry for the last ten years and travel full-time, writing, speaking, and leading worship together. They minister very often to families considering abortion, helping them feel safe and supported enough to choose to parent, with a firm belief in the importance of teaching about the family unit. Brandi does professional life coaching and is a dog trainer, and believes that all dogs deserve a chance. The Cunninghams are based out of Tennessee and have four dogs and incredible sons.

To contact the Cunninghams, visit www.FiresideGrace.com.

More Books by Fireside Grace:

The Dream Symbol Guide

Do you ever wonder what your dreams mean?

The parabolic language of dreams has long since been a mystery. Dreams invoke a thirst for supernatural understanding, and oftentimes lead many into new levels of spiritual awareness. With the plethora of dream symbols, dictionaries, and teachers, Brandi and Robyn saw a need for a Christian dream dictionary that would not only give an answer for what a symbol means, but would also give instructions about how to discern the meaning of dream symbols and equip readers to rely on the Holy Spirit to help interpret their dreams.

The Dream Symbol Guide unpacks thirteen different categories of symbols, with hundreds of entries covering many common and unique things that are in people's dreams, along with helpful teaching and perspective from Robyn and Brandi to assist you on the journey of understanding your dreams.

For more information, visit www.FiresideGrace.com.

More Books by Fireside Grace:

The Character of Christ

What is character, and why is it of utmost importance? Why take time to learn and go through an entire Bible study on this topic?

Character, in its simplest form, is the display of who we are when put under fire, or to the test. As we will learn together throughout this study, when we are put to the test is when we typically see the fruit of who we are shining brightly. The Bible makes it clear that it is important for us to, "bear good fruit," and to be ready to bear good fruit in season and out of season. This makes sense because this aligns with the character of Christ. He bore healthy fruit for all to see at all times and persevered through the fieriest of the trials a human could face. He showed us that we too possess the ability to remain the same yesterday, today, and tomorrow, despite the trials and circumstances that may arise. Matt. 7:18, "A good tree cannot bear bad fruit, and a bad tree cannot bear good fruit." Trees represent leadership symbolically. We need to be rooted to produce good fruit and the fruit of the spirit to harvest the souls that are beginning to come to us in waves. Join myself and the remnant as we grow and become strong enough in Jesus to press on through any amount of persecution that is here or may come.

For more information, visit www.FiresideGrace.com.

Why Choose Life Coaching?

As a life coach, Brandi Cunningham's job is to motivate you and help you develop the skills that it takes to continually stay motivated, even when no ones there to motivate you.

Maybe you don't know your purpose, or your calling. But just because it's not clear to you, doesn't mean you don't have one. Everyone has one!

Maybe you know your passion and calling but are not seeing the results you want because you're only able to halfheartedly devote your life to your calling, all the while feeling social and economic pressure to make money to pay the bills.

I'm here to help you save energy and time so that you can use it more on what you're passionate about, until you can do your passion, FULL TIME!

You see, you're unique. You have been made with skills are passions I do not have, and I need you—the world needs you. I won't just stand by and watch people die inside to depression, suicide, or anger because they had no one to help show them the way.

I'm here to help show you, and help you walk in that way. You can do this! Will you let us help?

Go to www.firesidegrace.com/shop to sign up today.

God Considered where He would place you before He even created you. Where you are at is where you will be most effective for His Kingdom.
May His face shine on you.

Jaclyn J.
Ryan